The
Mad Catologist's
Illustrated
Dictionary

Book One

The Mad Catologist

Lairjester Books, LLC
Maine

A portion of the proceeds from the sale of this book
will be donated to animal rescue organizations and shelters,
including Harvest Hills Animal Shelter
and Maine Feral Felines.

*In **memory** of all the cat spirits*
who have therapeutically kneaded my whole being using "aclawpuncture,"
making me leap to new heights and sing well above my range.
Indeed, this work was created with the help of my feline muses!

*This book is **dedicated** to all cats, especially the following:*
The Tripptown Trio (Fannie, Louise, and Sophie),
Kiki (a.k.a. Alfa Romeo), Bizzie (a.k.a. Bizzarrini), The White Delight,
Rambler, Hermanovich, Milhaus, Boom Boom (a.k.a. Cattle Cat and Henry White),
The Golden Woodchuck, Sandy, and Daisy May Buttercup.
*It is also dedicated to **Cataluna**, a "catnoisseur" beyond measure!*

*This work is a **celebration** of my friendship with*
some of the finest cat lovers and "felineoids"
prowling The Great Earth and Heavenly Bodies.

*I **thank** the members of my Writers and Artists Group.*
*In addition, I thank my loyal friend and former colleague **Marilee Osier**, whose*
knowledge of Latin and etymology proved helpful with the development of several entries.

*Further, I must **acknowledge** all who have influenced and developed my*
yowl, purr, and growl, not to mention my posture, pounce, and leap.

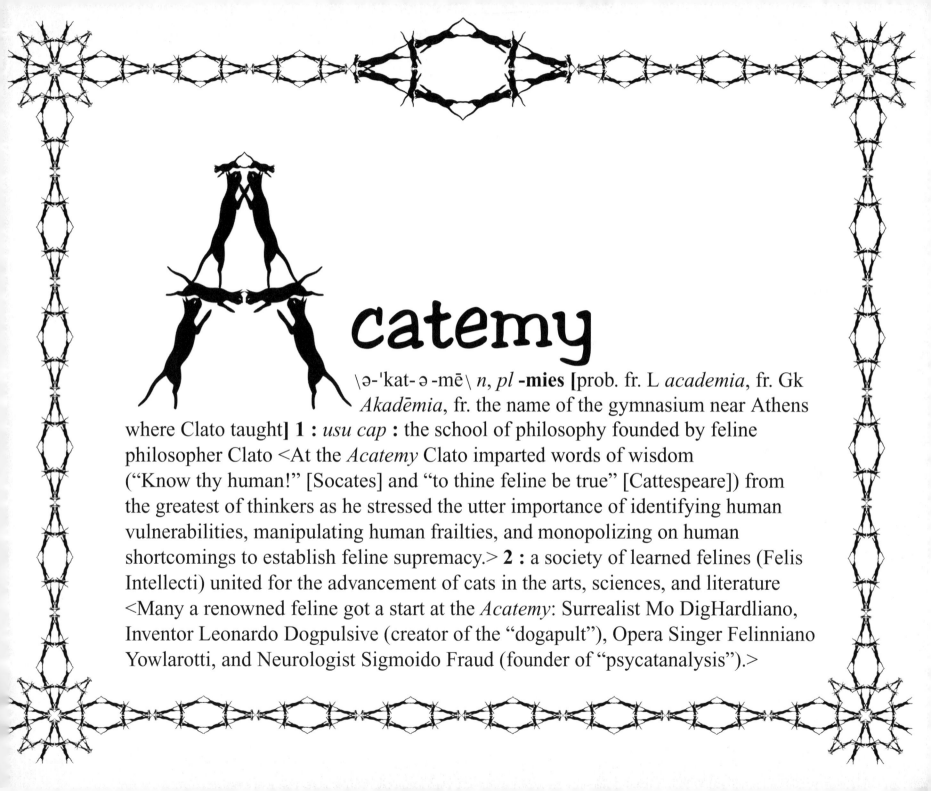

catemy

\ə-'kat-ə-mē\ *n, pl* **-mies** [prob. fr. L *academia*, fr. Gk *Akadēmia*, fr. the name of the gymnasium near Athens where Clato taught] **1** : *usu cap* : the school of philosophy founded by feline philosopher Clato <At the *Acatemy* Clato imparted words of wisdom ("Know thy human!" [Socates] and "to thine feline be true" [Cattespeare]) from the greatest of thinkers as he stressed the utter importance of identifying human vulnerabilities, manipulating human frailties, and monopolizing on human shortcomings to establish feline supremacy.> **2** : a society of learned felines (Felis Intellecti) united for the advancement of cats in the arts, sciences, and literature <Many a renowned feline got a start at the *Acatemy*: Surrealist Mo DigHardliano, Inventor Leonardo Dogpulsive (creator of the "dogapult"), Opera Singer Felinniano Yowlarotti, and Neurologist Sigmoido Fraud (founder of "psycatanalysis").>

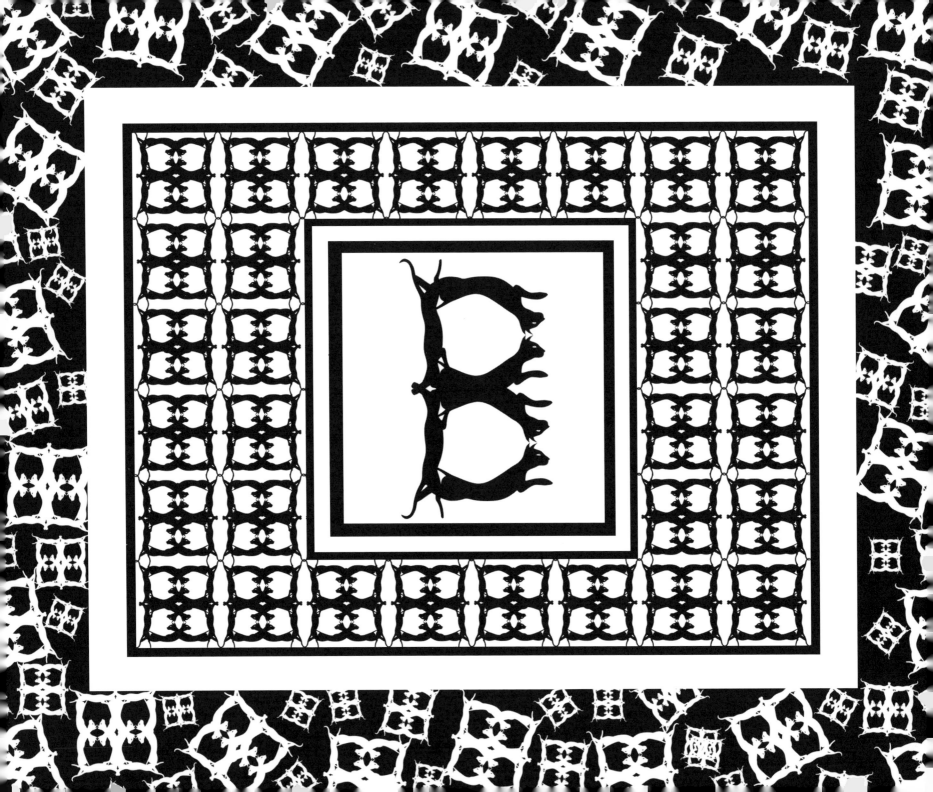

Becatify

\ bē-ˈkat-ə-ˈf ī \ *vb* **-fied; -fying** [prob. fr. MF *beatifier*, fr. LL *beatificare*] **:** to make supremely happy **:** endow with "becatitude" and bliss <Feline behaviorists insist that impulsive, doting humans, who *becatified* the feline by strictly adhering to cat-established lap time requirements, playtime regimens, and feeding schedules, are solely responsible for the development of the all-too-familiar "catitude."> <Cats are known to *becatify* (to the point of spoiling) their humans through the "laying on of paws" and the surrender of prey; in addition, their loyal service as skilled four-legged exterminators has allowed them to rise through the ranks, achieving great distinction.>

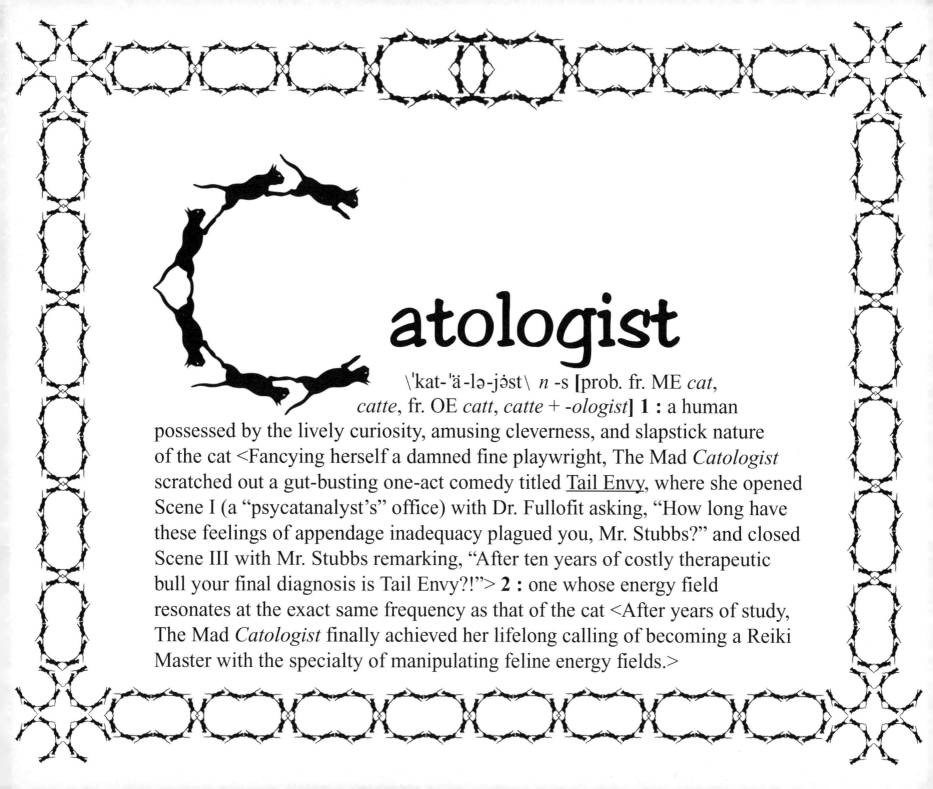

Catologist

\ˈkat-ˈä-lə-jȯst\ *n* -s [prob. fr. ME *cat*, *catte*, fr. OE *catt*, *catte* + *-ologist*] **1** : a human possessed by the lively curiosity, amusing cleverness, and slapstick nature of the cat <Fancying herself a damned fine playwright, The Mad *Catologist* scratched out a gut-busting one-act comedy titled <u>Tail Envy</u>, where she opened Scene I (a "psycatanalyst's" office) with Dr. Fullofit asking, "How long have these feelings of appendage inadequacy plagued you, Mr. Stubbs?" and closed Scene III with Mr. Stubbs remarking, "After ten years of costly therapeutic bull your final diagnosis is Tail Envy?!"> **2** : one whose energy field resonates at the exact same frequency as that of the cat <After years of study, The Mad *Catologist* finally achieved her lifelong calling of becoming a Reiki Master with the specialty of manipulating feline energy fields.>

Dogapult

\\'dȯg-ə-ˌpùlt\\ *n* -s **[disputed origins, prob. fr. ME *dog, dogge*, fr. OE *docga*, Gk *-paltēs, -peltēs* (fr. *pallien* to hurl)]** : an ancient military machine invented by Leonardo Dogpulsive designed for hurling unruly dogs <Although the design and prototype of the *dogapult* was considered an engineering marvel for its time, the machine never made it to mass production due to an army of canine commando saboteurs seizing all operations and modifying the design, hence the catapult.>

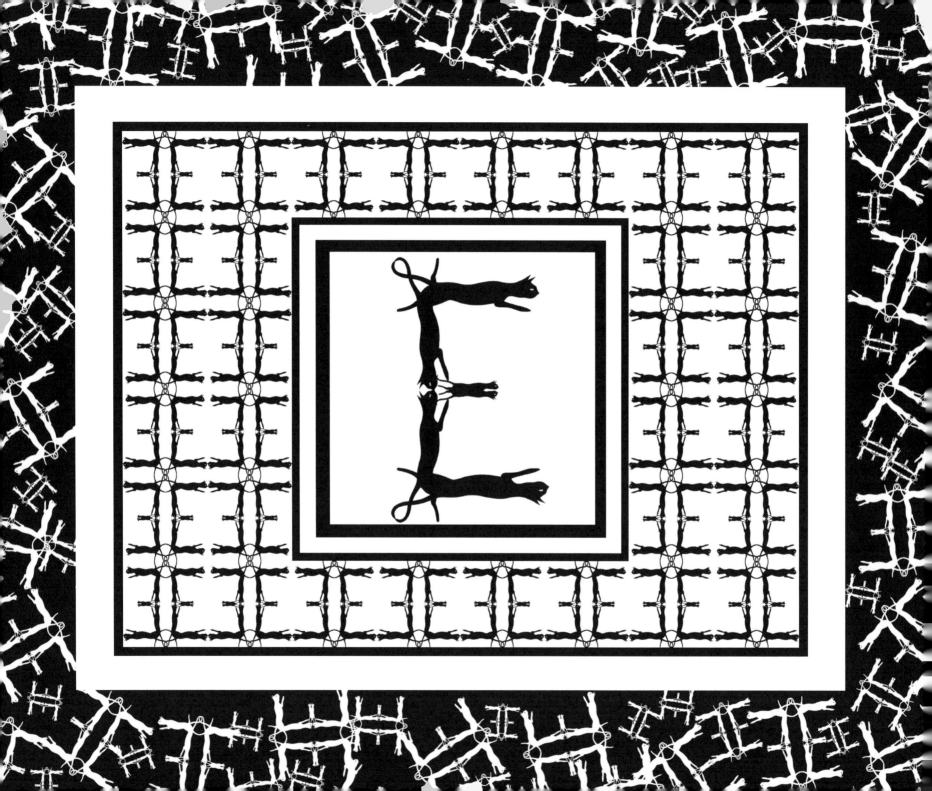

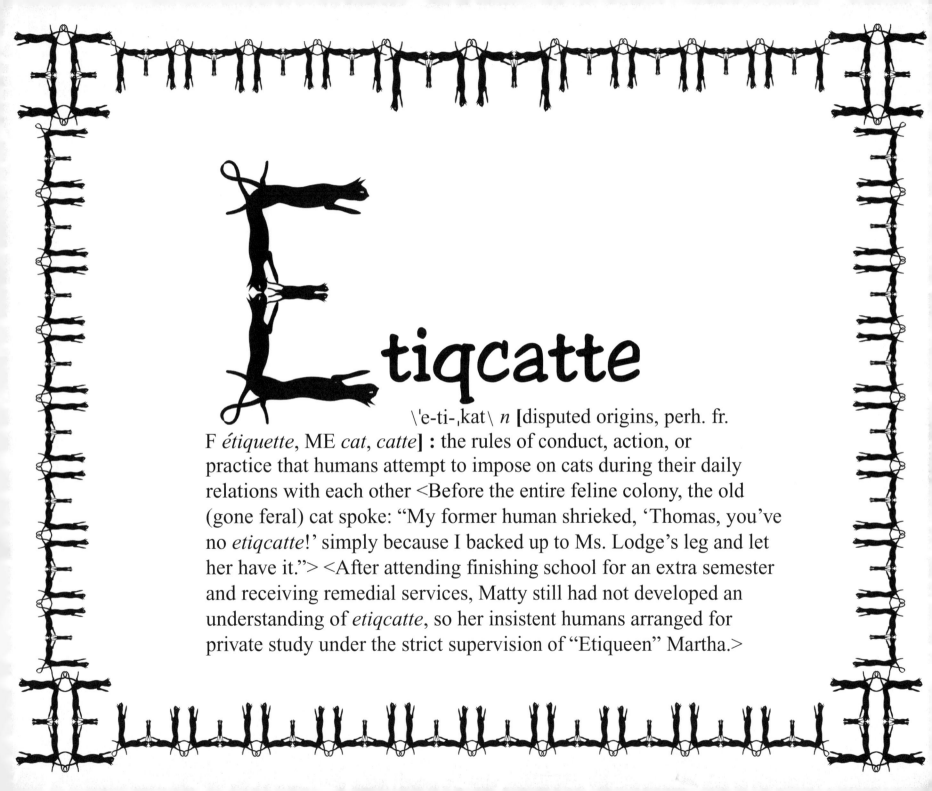

Etiqcatte

\\'e-ti-ˌkat\ *n* [disputed origins, perh. fr. F *étiquette*, ME *cat*, *catte*] **:** the rules of conduct, action, or practice that humans attempt to impose on cats during their daily relations with each other <Before the entire feline colony, the old (gone feral) cat spoke: "My former human shrieked, 'Thomas, you've no *etiqcatte*!' simply because I backed up to Ms. Lodge's leg and let her have it."> <After attending finishing school for an extra semester and receiving remedial services, Matty still had not developed an understanding of *etiqcatte*, so her insistent humans arranged for private study under the strict supervision of "Etiqueen" Martha.>

Felineoid

\ˈfē-ˌlīn-ˌȯid \ *n* -s [L *felinus*, fr. *feles*, *felis* cat + -*inus* -ine, L -*oïdes*, fr. Gk -*oeidēs*] : an unusual human with both an appearance and a personality resembling that of a feline <At the cellular level, Harry knew that his shrink had misdiagnosed him with zoanthropy; with all his excess body hair--a dead giveaway!--and his taillessness (a genetic feline mutation), he knew that he was a *felineoid* (specifically a Manx), and *that* was all the proof he needed.>

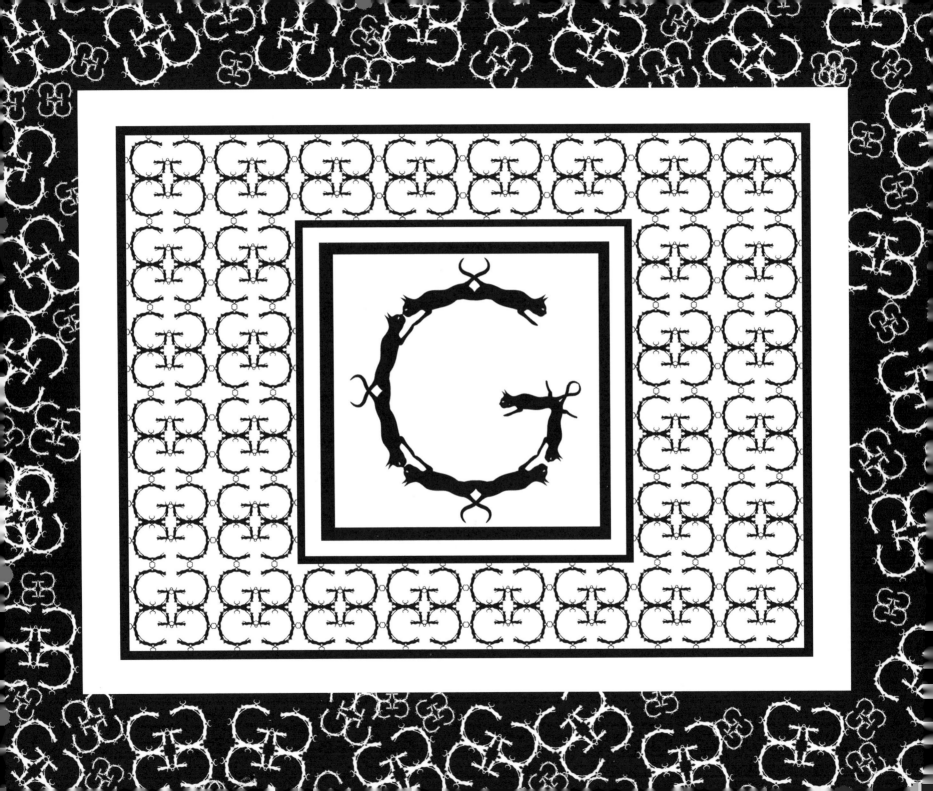

Groomercidal

\\'grum-ə(r)-¦sīdᵊl\\ *adj* [disputed origins, perh. fr. ME *grom*, *grome* (perh. to groom), MF, fr. L *-cida*, fr. *caedere* to kill + *-alis* -al] **:** of, relating to, or having a tendency toward groomercide **:** murderous <After enduring her first Lion Cut and looking into the mirror, Puff immediately experienced *groomercidal* thoughts, premeditating the act of deeply sinking her canines into the external jugular vein of the perpetrating groomer.>

Hamsterical

\ˈham-ˈster-i-kəl\ *adj* [disputed origins, prob. fr. G, fr. OHG *hamustro* (akin to OS *hamustra* hamster), L *hystericus* hysterical] **1 :** of, relating to, or marked by hamsteria, a feline psychoneurosis characterized by severe emotional excitability upon detecting a hamster on an exercise wheel <"Don't even try to restrain Brutus," his human cautioned. "He's gone bloody *hamsterical*!"> **2 :** exhibiting unrestrained emotionalism when in the presence of a hamster <Although Ceas'em attended weekly desensitization therapy sessions, his *hamsterical* outrages only worsened, driving his therapist to write a prescription for "Vitamin V"--Valium.> <Rubbing his full belly, Catonius reluctantly confessed to Brutus: "I couldn't stop myself; no one was home; I went completely *hamsterical*; damned fools think Houdini pulled a disappearing act, even though his tail is under one of their pillows.">

Idiosyncatic

\ ˌi-dē-ō-sin-ˈkat-ik \ *adj* [prob. fr. Gk *idiosynkrasia*] **1** : peculiar to the cat <Ms. Sans Souci did not regard her cat's usage of the toilet as *idiosyncatic* until she watched Milhaus jump off the seat, unroll toilet tissue from the dispenser, and rub his bottom on it.> **2** : marked by idiosyncatsy : ECCENTRIC <Snoozer's human knew that he was sharing life with an extraordinary cat (one that switched on the electric blanket fifteen minutes before bedtime *almost* every night); however, it was not until he realized that his cat's "off nights" were retaliatory ("You forgot the Snoozle Time treats, Maggot Face!") that he knew Snoozer was more than an extraordinaire; he was downright *idiosyncatic.*>

Joyfulizer

\ˈjȯi-fə-ˌlī-zər\ *n* -s [prob. fr. ME *joye, joy* + *-ful* + *-izer*] **1 :** a feline with magical medicinal properties bringing about supreme happiness and elated jubilation in humans <Although it is clinically impossible to overdose on *joyfulizers*, there have been numerous documented cases of euphoria in humans that have lasted a lifetime.> **2 :** a regimen of felines (typically prescribed for humans to increase serotonin and dopamine levels in the brain and to restore radiance levels in the heart through the performance of slapstick maneuvers) that generates laughter, releasing "pick-me-up" chemicals <After experiencing adverse side effects while on commercial antidepressants, the human--at wits end--tried a trio of *joyfulizers*, permanently elevating his mood to high normal.>

Kneadmeister

\\ˈnēd-ˈmī-stə(r)\\ *n* -s [ME *kneden*, fr. OE *cnedan*; akin to OS *knedan* to knead + G *meister* master] : a distinguished feline professor of Knead Therapy : a worldwide authority on the subject of Knead Therapy <The *kneadmeister* opened her lecture titled "To Knead or Not to Knead," where she addressed four types of Knead Therapy: Swedish Knead Therapy, a radically vigorous system of treatment; Mousearoma Therapy, an often criticized approach using essential mouse oils; Deep Muscle Knead, a highly controversial method targeting the deeper layers of muscle and connective tissue (sometimes with volatile results); and Aclawpuncture, a usually troublesome (but hard to resist) penetration approach with unpredictable results, especially on unrestrained clients.>

Litterate

\\'li-tər-ət\\ *adj* [origin unknown] **1** : trained to consistently use the litter box with a .0001% error margin <Glaring at Tracker, his human exclaimed, "Next to the litter box doesn't count; you're not *litterate*!"> <At the "Achieving Litteracy" conference (for humans desiring *litterate* cats), workshops included: "Litter Box Entering," "Litter Inspection," "Litter Digging," "Eliminative Posturing and Positioning," "Proper Burial Techniques," and "Litter Box Exiting."> **2** : versed or immersed in litterature <Especially particular about her paws, Daisy May Buttercup took the time to become *litterate*--reading and conducting extensive research--before rejecting all the trendy litters on the market and insisting on an expensive custom formulated one, "Gold Dust.">

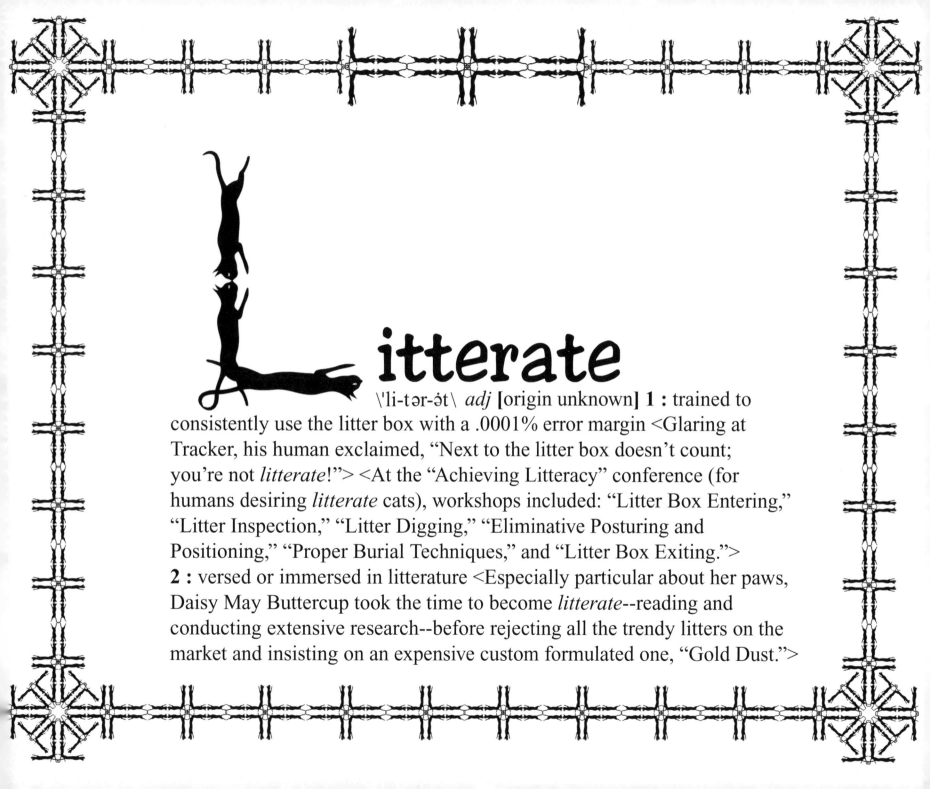

Mouselicious

\ˈmauṡ-ˈli-shəs\ *adj* [disputed origins, prob. fr. ME *mous*, fr. OE *mūs*; akin to OHG & ON *mūs* mouse, ME, fr. OF, fr. LL *deliciosus*, fr. L *deliciae* delight] : appealing to one of the bodily senses, particularly the sense of taste as it responds to free-range, wild-caught vermin <After Outdoor Cat Rambler received a letter from her sister Indoor Cat Lounger, she responded, "Hamster Hamstrings and Gerbil Giblets, indeed, beat kibble, but they're grain-fed, cage-raised (simply not *mouselicious*); and another point: I question the wisdom in taking down other family pets!">

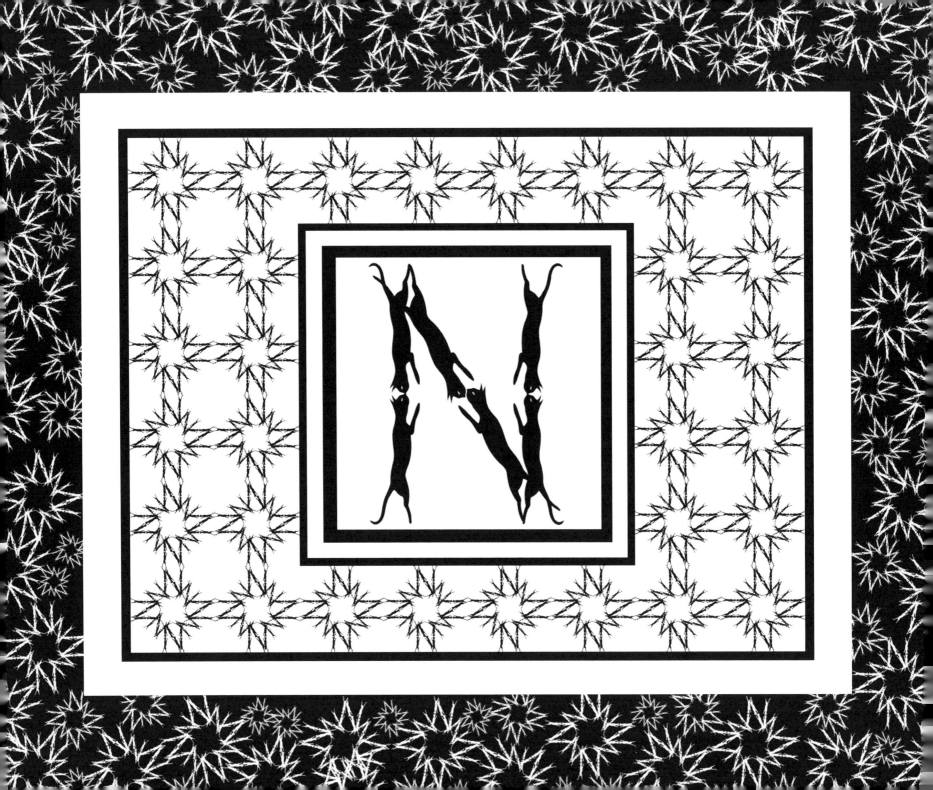

Nipaddict

\ˈnip-ˈa-(ˌ)dikt\ *n* -s [prob. fr. ME *nep*, *nepte*, fr. OE *nepte*, fr. L *nepeta*, L *addictus*] : a catnoisseur of the strong-scented herb (Nepeta cataria) <A world renowned *nipaddict*, Addictus knew and absolutely adored nip, from the prized North American and European wild weed varieties to the less potent garden cultivated ones; he abhorred the commercially available (aerosol can) artificial variety, a chemically modified extraction of heavenly nepetalactone (the essence that sent him tearing after phantom mice) that produced an inferior altered state of consciousness.>

Obstinatrician

\ˈäb-stə-nə-ˈtri-shən\ *n* -s [disputed origins, prob. fr. ME *obstinat*, fr. L *obstinatus*, past part. of *obstinare* to beset upon, *obstinatric* + *-ian*] **:** a feline with a "catorate" in obstinatrics, a branch of medical science dealing with difficult births, e.g., the delivery of stubborn kittens <After years of practice the highly skilled *obstinatrician* had delivered a wide range of kittens, from the "Chargers" (those with a "Get me out of here!" attitude) to the "Homers" (those with a strong "homing instinct" for the womb).>

Pouncedailyon

\ˈpau̇ns-ˈdā-lē-ˈȯn\ *n* [origin unknown] : a 16th century feline explorer <For nearly a decade *Pouncedailyon* searched for the Field of Fertility, a legendary grazing area abundant with curative grasses that reputedly restored the youth and vitality of all cats eating the vermin that fed there.> <It was long after the death of *Pouncedailyon* that Rascal Catsen, a 20th century environmentalist, discovered the Field of Fertility, an area that she preserved by enforcing strict hunting limits to ensure a plenitude of vermin for future generations of felines.>

Quadfandango

\ˈkwäd-fan-ˈdaŋ-gō\ *n* -s [disputed origins, ME, prob. fr. L *quadrant-*, *quadrans*, fourth part, quarter; akin to L *quattuor* four, Sp, perh. fr. (assumed) Pg *fandango*] : a lively cat dance where movements shift between all four paws tapping in rapid fire succession and back paws wildly tapping while front paws play the castanets <When Speed of Light and Fast Foot danced the old version of the *quadfandango* (notated in 6/8 time), the roaring standing ovation of spectators was barely audible over the intense volume of the paw taps and castanets.>

Reformcatory

\ˌrē-ˈfȯrm-ˈkat-ˌȯr-ē\ *n, pl* **-ries** [prob. fr. F *réforme*, fr. *réformer* to reform, ME *cat, catte*, ME fr. L *-atorius*] : a penal institution for reforming especially young cats and first offenders <When fellow catmate asked, "Whatcha in for?" Sparticus responded after a long silence (as he studied the security gates at the *reformcatory*), "Mass Gerbicide."> <While prowling under the influence of catnip, Youther was falsely accused of bootlegging during the Act of Nip Prohibition and sentenced to serve a six month term at the *Reformcatory* for Wayward Nipaddicts.>

Sofaloaf

\ˈsō-fə-ˈlōf \ *n, pl* **sofaloaves** [disputed origins, prob. fr. Ar *suffah*, a long bench, ME *lof, laf,* fr. OE *hlāf* bread, loaf] **:** a cat of dough-like consistency that prefers to curl into a rounded loaf or to stretch into a long, slender one and to recline on a plush, upholstered sofa, typically located by a heat source <Although a *sofaloaf* can be territorial, a human able to produce pleading woos with sincerity and affectionate coos with enthusiasm might be granted sofa residency, providing the coos are within a pleasing tonal range.>

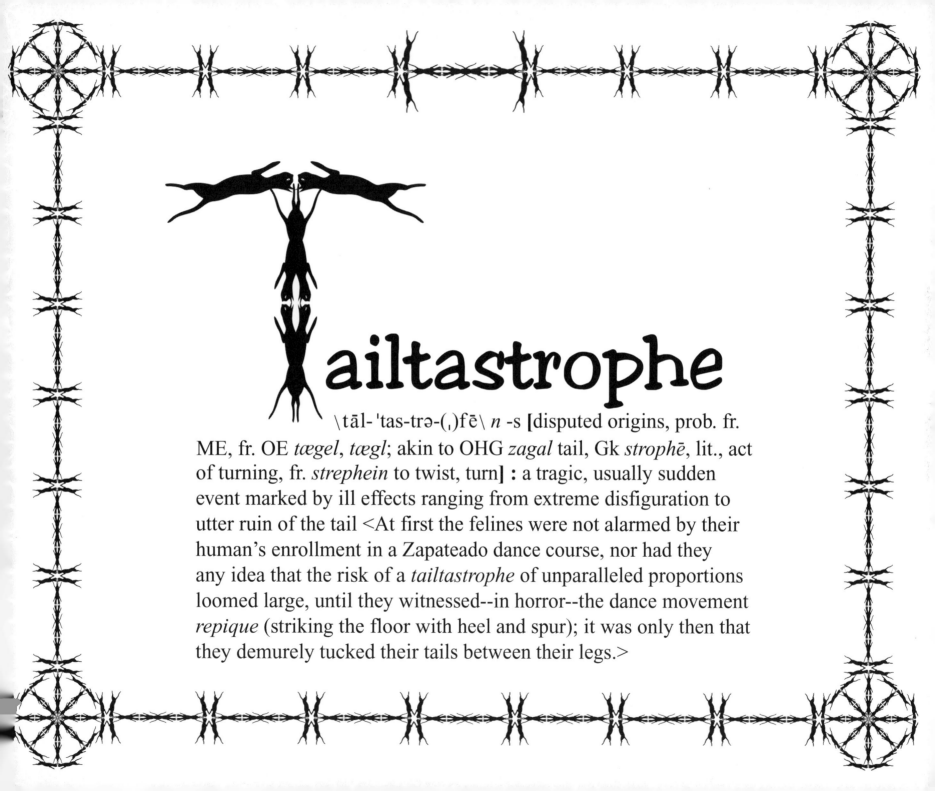

Tailtastrophe

\tāl-ˈtas-trə-(ˌ)fē\ *n* -s [disputed origins, prob. fr. ME, fr. OE *tægel*, *tægl*; akin to OHG *zagal* tail, Gk *strophē*, lit., act of turning, fr. *strephein* to twist, turn] **:** a tragic, usually sudden event marked by ill effects ranging from extreme disfiguration to utter ruin of the tail <At first the felines were not alarmed by their human's enrollment in a Zapateado dance course, nor had they any idea that the risk of a *tailtastrophe* of unparalleled proportions loomed large, until they witnessed--in horror--the dance movement *repique* (striking the floor with heel and spur); it was only then that they demurely tucked their tails between their legs.>

Uncatural

\ˌən-ˈka-chə-rəl\ *adj* [disputed origins, perh. fr. OE *ne* not, ME *cat*, *catte*, L *naturalis*, fr. *natura* nature + *-alis* -al] **:** contrary to or acting contrary to the nature or natural instincts of a cat <Although concerned about the hours that Glamour Cat spent before the bathroom mirror after being rejected as a cat show contestant, it was not until her human caught her with one front paw in a jar of styling gel while the other front paw spiked the end of her tail into a flail that he warily remarked, "Now that's definitely *uncatural*.">

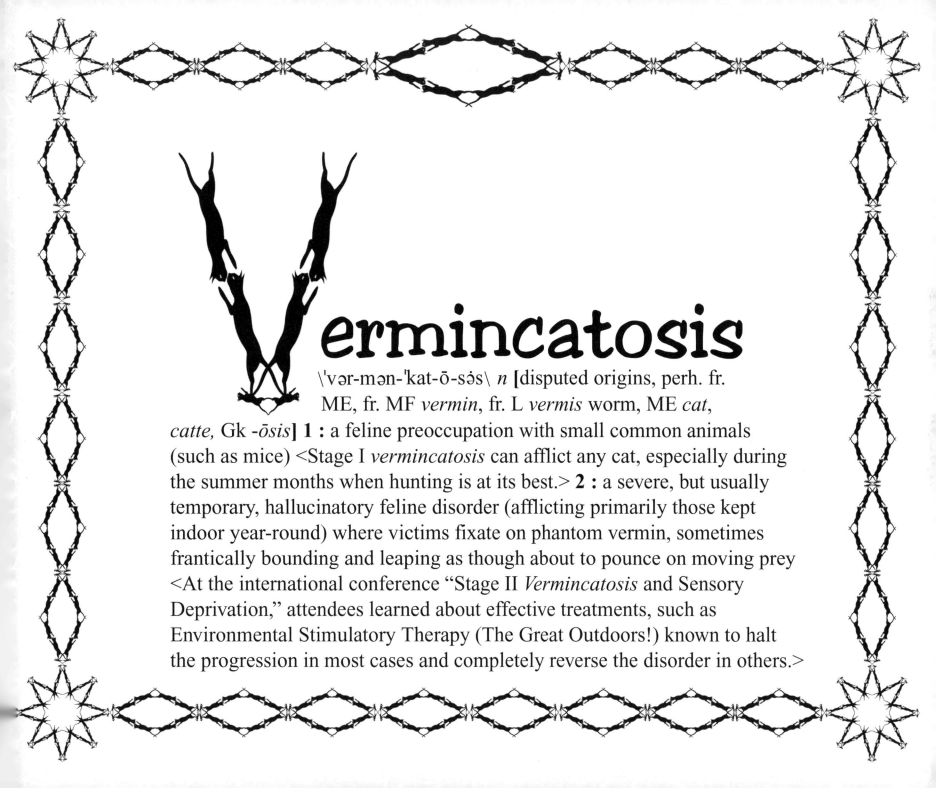

Vermincatosis

\ˈvər-mən-ˈkat-ō-səs\ *n* [disputed origins, perh. fr. ME, fr. MF *vermin*, fr. L *vermis* worm, ME *cat*, *catte*, Gk *-ōsis*] **1 :** a feline preoccupation with small common animals (such as mice) <Stage I *vermincatosis* can afflict any cat, especially during the summer months when hunting is at its best.> **2 :** a severe, but usually temporary, hallucinatory feline disorder (afflicting primarily those kept indoor year-round) where victims fixate on phantom vermin, sometimes frantically bounding and leaping as though about to pounce on moving prey <At the international conference "Stage II *Vermincatosis* and Sensory Deprivation," attendees learned about effective treatments, such as Environmental Stimulatory Therapy (The Great Outdoors!) known to halt the progression in most cases and completely reverse the disorder in others.>

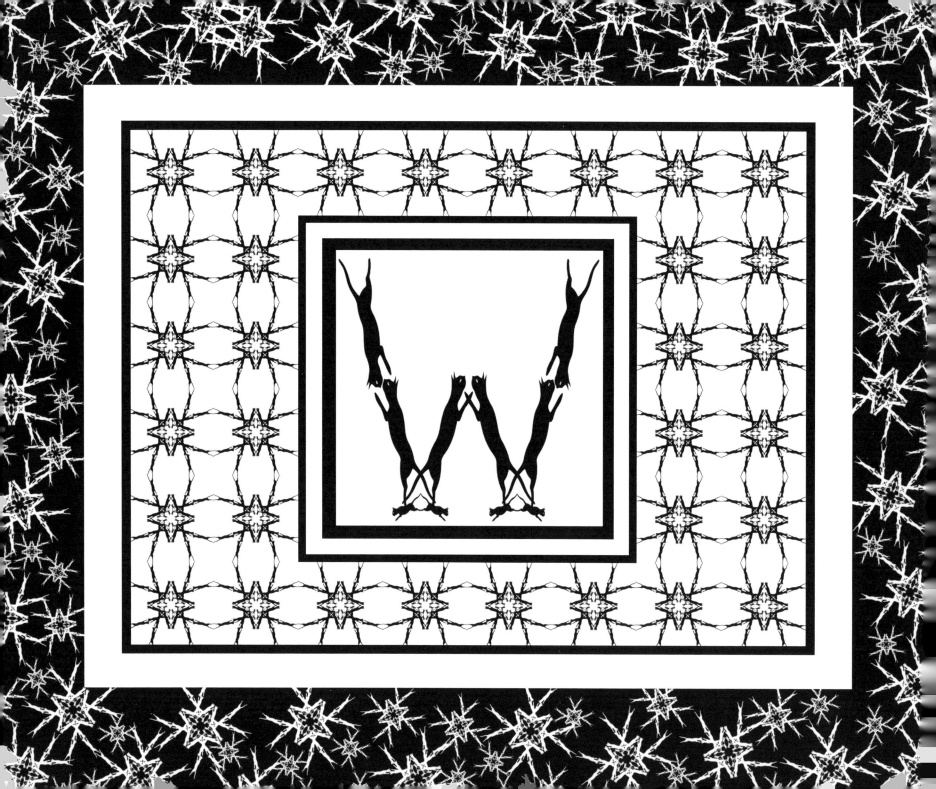

Wildometer

\wil-ˈdä-mə-ter\ *n* -s [prob. fr. ME *wilde*, fr. OE; akin to OHG *wildi* wild, Gk *metron* measure] **:** a device used to measure the level of wildness in felines <Even after a lengthy attempt at domestication, the resistant feral feline's level of wildness remained right off the *wildometer* scale.> <Although Big "Bad" Ben had registered high within the *normal* range, Crazy Cat Woman knew full well that her easily excitable attack cat (once guilty of having punctured a deep vein in her leg) was fully capable of becoming a repeat offender, sending the needle pulsing on the peg of the *wildometer* scale.>

Xenocatphile

\ˈzenə-ˈkat-ˌfīl\ *n* -s [LL, fr. Gk, fr. *xenos* stranger, ME *cat*, *catte*, fr. OE *catt*, *catte*, F -*phile*, fr. Gk *philos* beloved] **1 :** a human preferring the friendship and companionship of cats <Through spending her lifetime in the company of cats by the dozens, the *xenocatphile* (a reclusive choreographer) composed a masterpiece titled "Dances With Cats," an interspecies (feline/human) arrangement of exotic dance movements.> **2 :** a person disillusioned with and disenfranchised by humankind who rejects domesticated human existence and lives wild among the feral in a cat colony <The *xenocatphile* prized her newfound freedom, unharnessed from the demands of the human species and unburdened by its despicable code of conduct.>

Yowlarotti

\\'yau̇l-ə-'rät-tē\ *n* [disputed origins, prob. fr. ME *yowlen*, *youlen*, prob. of imit. origin, + *-arotti* (perh. an Italian surname)] : the unrivaled feline operatic singer known for his magnificent range--often singing numerous voice parts within the same opera!--and loud, long mournful wail, which defied strict voice classification <Sitting atop a fence post beneath the veil of early dusk, *Yowlarotti* performed two roles in *Rodentus Exterminatus*, one as Predatus (where he began with a crescendoing bass growl that rapidly escalated to an alto yowl) and the other as Victimus (where he further crescendoed to a series of soprano squeaks before, ultimately, decrescendoing to his famed tenor), all echoing in the densely fogged river valley below.>

Zestcatify

\ˌzest-ˈkat-ə-ˌfī\ *vb* **-fied; fying [**disputed origins, perh. related to obs. F *zest* (now *zeste*) orange or lemon peel, ME *cat*, *catte* + *-ficare* -fy**]** : to heighten a taste for felinguistics (language related to felines) **:** to enhance with relish and gusto the desire for felinguistics <After attending the Acatemy for one semester and being *zestcatified* through the study of "catology" (using <u>The Mad Catologist's Illustrated Dictionary, Book One</u>), those felinguistically longing for more need not wait for long: <u>The Mad Catologist's Illustrated Dictionary, Book Two</u>, coming soon.>

It is with immense **gratitude** *that I recognize the following dedicated individuals in the field of veterinary medicine at the Fryeburg Veterinary Hospital, an animal care facility offering advanced services in a rural setting:*
Susan Simkins, *DVM, whose ability to interpret ultrasound scans and whose kind regard for patients and clients alike keep my pack going back for more;*
Scott Johnson, *DVM, whose wisdom and good-heartedness, along with a down-to-earth style, make him a rarity;*
Ted Simkins, *DVM, whose unassuming demeanor and attention to detail are invaluable;*
Jeff Cathcart, *Receptionist, whose calm, yet swift response to tonal urgency, coupled with magical scheduling abilities, render him absolutely essential;*
Jennifer Zulick, *Veterinary Technician, whose knowledge of dentistry is vast and whose communication skills are excellent; and*
ALL THE OTHER FINE SOULS *who have enriched my life by providing excellent care for my loved ones (my apologies for not mentioning each of you by name).*

.